Knots & Ropes
for Climbers

Knots & Ropes for Climbers

Duane Raleigh

Illustrations by Mike Clelland

STACKPOLE
BOOKS

Published by
STACKPOLE BOOKS
5067 Ritter Road
Mechanicsburg, PA 17055
www.stackpolebooks.com

Printed in the United States

10 9 8

First edition

Cover design by Caroline Stover

Library of Congress Cataloging-in-Publication Data
Raleigh, Duane.
    Knots and Ropes for Climbers / Duane Raleigh.
        p. cm.
    ISBN 0-8117-2871-4
    1. Climbing Knots. 2. Knots and Splices. Title.
GV200.19.K56R35 1998   97-22467
796.52'2—dc21   CIP

ISBN 978-0-8117-2871-3

Contents

"The camel is the most ruminative of animals,
and he slobbers constantly while he ruminates, particularly
on his Picket-Line Hitch, which he believes is provided
for this purpose. His knot is always sopping,
but it has been very nicely planned; and so, wet or dry,
it is never difficult to untie and it does not slip
in either direction."

—Clifford W. Ashley
The Ashley Book of Knots, 1944

1

About Knots

We cannot safely climb without rope. And we cannot use rope without knots. Knots, like life, are slippery devils, full of twists and complications. Both are unforgiving. Make one wrong turn, and the whole mess falls apart. Or you find yourself wrapped in a hairy snarl.

Unlike life, however, you can practice tying knots. You can grab a hank of line and run the rabbit out of the hole, around the tree, and back into the hole until you can render the Bowline perfect every time.

Even if we didn't climb mountains, we would never get far without knots. About three steps, and our shoes would fall off. So we must master at least one knot or go barefoot. Things get a tad more complex when we climb. For that activity, you have the Ring Bend, Prusik, Figure Eight, Bowline, Grapevine, Klemheist—the list is near endless.

But you need not know every hitch and bend to climb safely or well. What follows are instructions for a variety of knots that I've found useful throughout twenty-four years of climbing. For simplicity, I've weeded out the superfluous. Still, you will notice a number of redundancies. For example, the Figure Eight Follow-Through and the Double Bowline serve the same purpose—to join climber to rope—yet I've included both, when learning one would suffice. This is done not to confuse, but to give you a choice. I've climbed with hundreds of partners, and about half preferred the Bowline; the others swore by the Figure Eight. After you learn both, you will likely come to favor one over the other. Perhaps you'll find that the Bowline is easier to untie after it has held a hard jerk. Or you'll prefer the peace of mind and simplicity of the Figure Eight. I use both, depending on my mood.

Similarly, you'll find four ascending knots—the Prusik, Klemheist, Bachman, and Auto Block. All do essentially the same thing, but each has a distinct advantage over the others in certain situations. A smart climber will commit all four to memory. Various other overlaps occur throughout the book. This is intentional.

But you can't teach someone how to tie knots by written description alone. Take the humble Square Knot, for example. To tie, take hold of the rope or cord and grasp an end in each hand. Cross the right over the left, run it behind, then up through the forming loop. Now take the right strand (used to be the left strand), pass it around the left (used to be the right), run it behind, and then up through the forming loop. Pull both ends taut to dress. Do the second step backward, however, and you get the treacherous Granny Knot, which easily falls apart. See what I mean? And this was a simple knot. Try the same with the complex Bowline, and you could come untied from your climbing harness and pay a fast visit to the Almighty.

So how does a book teach knot tying? Through illustration. For that onerous task we've employed the gifts of the inkman Mike Clelland. He lives up in the rough mountains of Idaho and practices what he draws most every day. His scratch-pen drawings take you step by step through tying each knot. The words that follow are meant to provide insight into the knot's uses, and in some cases touch on the abstract. Study the illustrations, mouth the words, and you'll find that tying even the most roundabout knots is easy.

Of course, you should practice your knots somewhere other than on the cliff or mountain. Flat ground is good. A comfortable chair is ideal. Practice until there are no questions. Getting it right is an absolute. If you doubt your knot, it is wrong. Untie and go again. A properly tied knot will look right. It will not have odd crossings or twists.

When you are about to start a climb, have a trusted friend double-check your lashings. I've probably tied the Bowline ten thousand times, but I still get that bugger wrong now and then, usually when I'm caught up in jabber or debate, fogged by fear, or distracted by the bark of a mean dog. Having a friend examine my tie-in knot has saved my life at least once.

2

Knotty Words

The common definition for a *knot* is any complication in a rope or sling that isn't caused by accident. When you toss a rope off a route to rappel and the rope works itself into a bird's nest, it may seem like you have a knot, but all you really have is a problem. To untangle a snarl of this sort, keep the wad loose, and be patient. Usually the tail of the rope has not involved itself, so all you need to do is pull the loops apart. Rushing or pulling the end through, while satisfying, will only cost you more time.

In actual use, most people lump together hitches, bends, and everything else, including our tangle, and refer to all as knots. For demonstration purposes, however, it helps to be more specific, even if you forget the terminology as soon as the book cover snaps shut.

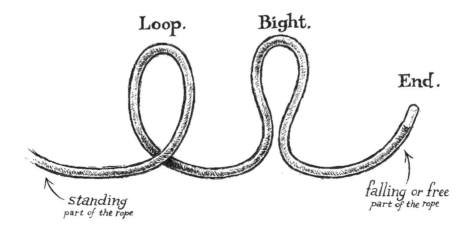

Loop. Bight. End.

standing
part of the rope

falling *or free*
part of the rope

Figure Eight.

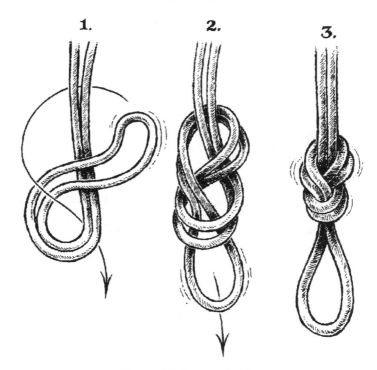

Figure Eight on a Bight.

The end of the rope is simply the *end*. The bit of rope that sticks out of the knot is the *tail*. The length of rope between the two ends is the *bight*. Any knot tied between the two ends is referred to as *on a bight*. A Figure Eight on a Bight, for example, is tied somewhere in the middle of the rope, as opposed to in an end, where it would be just a plain Figure Eight.

Cross a bight of rope over itself and you get a *loop*. The *working* section of rope is the one getting the knot, and the *standing* section is the inactive bit that doesn't have any knots tied in it.

A *hitch* ties a rope to an object, or another rope if that rope is stationary. Hitches are usually wrapped rather than knotted around an object. You hitch a horse to a post, a runner around a horn, a tie-off around a piton. A common climbing hitch is the Girth Hitch.

When you join rope to rope or webbing to webbing, you tie a *bend*. Popular climbing bends are the Ring Bend and the Double Fisherman's, which is still a bend even if its name doesn't say so.

Girth Hitch on a piton.

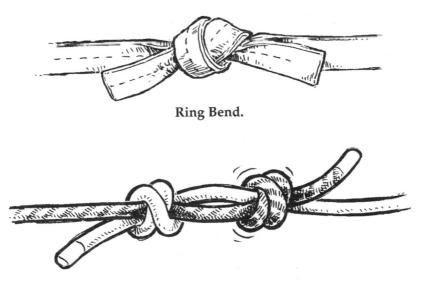

Ring Bend.

Double Fisherman's knot, about to be set.

Knots, hitches, and bends must be drawn up clean and snug to hold. *Drawing up* or *setting* the knot is critical. Leave a knot loose, and it is apt to come untied or pull apart when it suffers a load. Also, be neat and "dress" your knot so none of its parts are twisted or crossed over. A sloppily tied knot, besides being difficult to visually inspect, can slip or may even form a knot different from the one intended. Do it right and remember, "Not neat knots, need not be knotted." In most cases, you set a knot by working all its parts up tight, then tugging on the ends, or the end and the standing section.

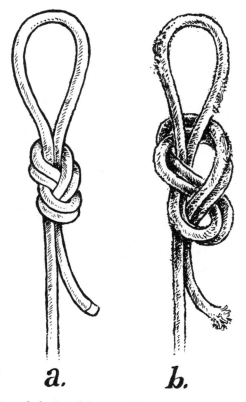

a.   b.

A properly set and dressed knot (a) looks neat and has all its parts pulled up snug. Leave a knot loose or sloppily tied (b), and it can come apart in a crisis.

3

Starter Knots

Figure Eight Follow-Through, prior to drawing up.

It's easy to be swallowed by the magnitude of the sport when you're first learning. How do cams work? Is this nut placed right? Is this my braking hand? Am I tied in right?

The best thing is to go slow. Learn the rudiments one at a time, then as you become expert in each of those, add the specialized. The process will continue forever; I've climbed for more than two decades and am still learning.

Where do you begin? You could climb forever knowing only five knots. The *Figure Eight Follow-Through* will work in all situations as your tie-in knot. A variation, the *Figure Eight Fisherman's*, will always work well to join rope to rope. The *Ring Bend* will secure webbing to webbing. You could leave it at that, but you would be ill prepared to improvise in an emergency or uncomfortable bind. For that reason, add the *Munter Hitch*, which serves as a rappel and belay knot, and the *Prusik*, the ascending knot, to your repertoire. Learn these five knots immediately. The others you can add as your experience grows and your confusion fades.

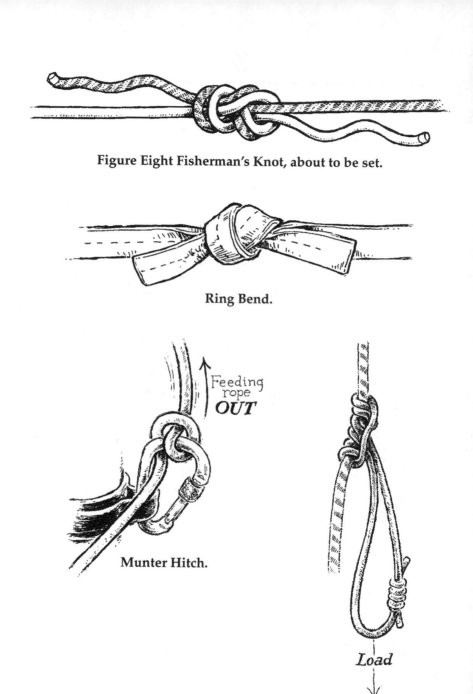

Figure Eight Fisherman's Knot, about to be set.

Ring Bend.

Feeding
rope
OUT

Munter Hitch.

Load

Prusik Knot.

4

Knots

You could make a life's work out of studying knots, as there are some thirty-nine hundred recorded. Fortunately, climbers need bother with only thirty-five, and that's not as bad as it sounds. Only nineteen are independent designs; the remaining sixteen are variations.

What follows are those knots and how-to illustrations. For most knots, common uses and secondary uses are given. The common uses are the ones the knots excel at. The secondary uses are those that will get you by, although I'd avoid them when possible, as there is nearly always a better knot for the job.

OVERHAND

The simple Overhand is probably among the first knots you learned as a child. It has a nostalgic appeal, but for climbing it is of minor value. Many climbers put it in the end of the belay rope to prevent dropping the leader should the rope's tail sneak up and try to slip through the belay device. For this use it's fine, as it's quick to tie even with one hand.

Overhand Knot.

Similarly, you can tie an Overhand in each end of your rappel rope to help prevent the tails from pulling through your rappel device. I've used the Overhand as a stopper knot once or twice in a rappel rope, but only when I was in a hurry or not thinking right. In clearer moments you'll find that the Double Overhand and special Stopper Knots work better, offering bulkier stoppers that are less likely to untie.

Common Use
• Stopper knot in the end of a belay rope

Secondary Use
• Stopper knot in the end of a rappel rope

DOUBLE OVERHAND
The Double Overhand is a more useful variation. This knot takes only one more turn to tie than the single but provides a bulkier stopper that is also less likely to untie itself. Outside the world of climbing, the Double Overhand is tied in the ends of whips to prevent unraveling and add spice to the taste of the lash.

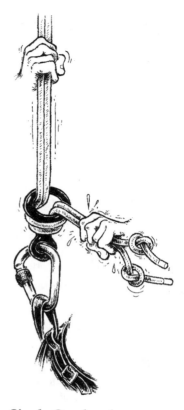

Single Overhands may slip through a rappel device.

Double Overhand Knot.

Common Uses
• Stopper knot in the end of a belay rope
• Stopper knot in the end of a rappel rope

OVERHAND ON A BIGHT

This version of the Overhand is the most misused of the climbing knots. Foolish climbers use it as a middleman's knot or to anchor the rope. In both cases, there are far better knots. Use the Overhand on a Bight for either purpose, and you'll quickly learn that it's about impossible to untie after it's held body weight, especially when the rope is wet.

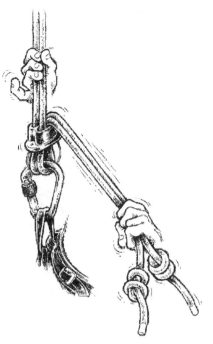

Double Overhands used as stopper knots in a rappeling device.

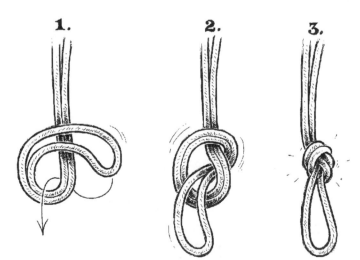

1. **2.** **3.**

Overhand on a Bight.

Tie the Overhand on a Bight near the end of the rappel rope, and you have the Overhand Loop, the best stopper knot I've found. Clip a carabiner through the loop and this knot is impossible to pull through any rappel device.

Common Use
• Excellent stopper knot in the end of a rappel rope

Secondary Uses
• Emergency tie-in
• Emergency anchor point

OVERHAND BEND

This bend, writes Clifford W. Ashley, "is used in joining the ends of rope yarns by which hams, bacon, and bananas are hung." Smart climbers avoid this knot when possible, which is most of the time when you must tie two ropes together. Still, the Overhand Bend has its uses. It's the fastest and simplest knot to tie rappel ropes together, admirable qualities when a storm is bearing down. Also, because both rope ends point in the same direction and the knot makes a trim bundle, it's the least likely knot to jam when it's dragged down the cliff during rope retrieval.

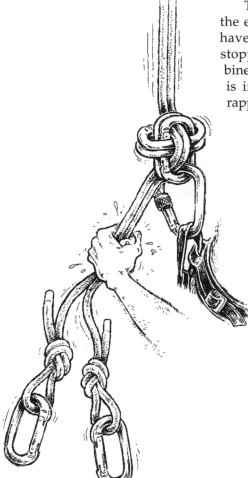

A rappel rope-stopper using carabiners in an Overhand on a Bight, a.k.a. the Overhand Loop.

In the Saxony region of Germany, where metal protection is banned by law to protect the soft sandstone, they tie the Overhand Bend in short runners and slings. These they then jam, stopper-style, in crack constrictions. The practice works amazingly well, so long as

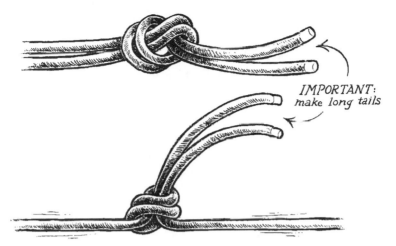

IMPORTANT:
make long tails

The Overhand Bend.

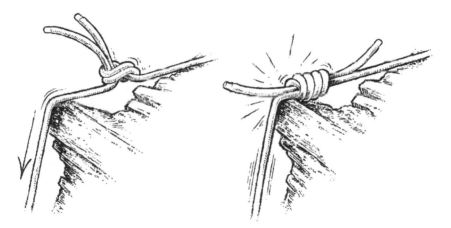

An Overhand Bend moves easily over edges (left) where other knots, like a Double Fisherman's, might tend to snag (right).

you keep the knot soft and flat when you lay it in the crack, then jerk it to cause it to swell. A thin stick is useful for poking the knot back into the crack. Use your jammed Overhand Bends as protection when the real thing isn't available, or to back up suspect rappel anchors.

In all uses of the Overhand Bend, take care to leave a 6-inch tail in each end, and don't use this bend to join ropes of drastically different diameters.

Common Use
• Joining rappel ropes

Secondary Use
• Improvised jammed-knot protection

OVERHAND FOLLOW-THROUGH

A few sport climbers use this knot to tie in to the rope. For that use, the Overhand Follow-Through is simple and safe, but it's difficult to untie after it has caught a fall. I suspect that most everyone would abandon this knot upon learning the superior Figure Eight Follow-Through or Double Bowline with Jack's Variation. Those who fail to see the light and persist with this arcane knot should leave a long tail in it and secure this with a Double Fisherman's.

Common Use
• Tying rope to harness

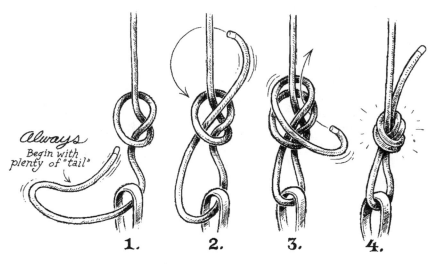

1.   2.   3.   4.

Overhand Follow-Through.

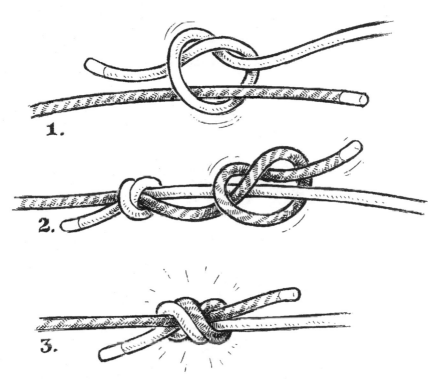

Single Fisherman's Knot.

SINGLE FISHERMAN'S

This knot—two Overhands laced through each other—is too likely to loosen and untie itself to be sound. Don't use it. This bastardization of the Double Fisherman's is shown here only because a well-versed climber should know which knots to avoid as well as which to use.

Common Use
• None

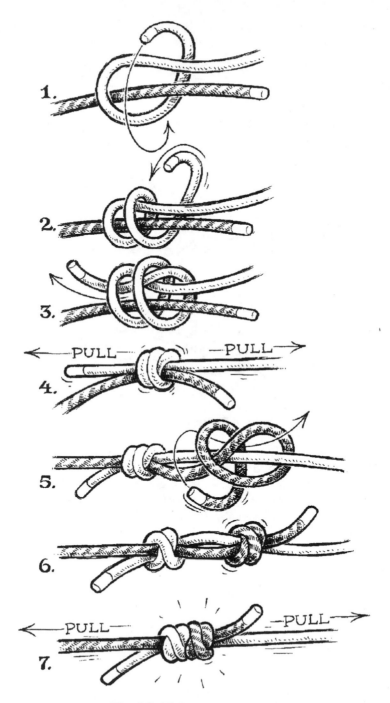

Double Fisherman's Knot.

DOUBLE FISHERMAN'S (GRAPEVINE)

As the name suggests, the Double Fisherman's is popular among anglers who don't want the big one to get away. This knot is famous for joining fishing line, but it works just as well to join two climbing ropes, although I believe the Figure Eight Follow-Through is safer because it's a simpler knot.

A better use of the Double Fisherman's is for tying cord that's slung through nuts. The knot also works for joining webbing, but I've never taken to it because I have a hard time getting the thing to look right. If you do use it for tying together either ropes or cord, make sure you keep the tails about 3 inches long.

Finally, tie one side of this knot in the end of a rope and it's a solid backup for most other knots. Though the Double Fisherman's is relegated to an ignominious position in the knot hierarchy, it's the best knot for securing the tails of all tie-in knots.

Harness ← tie-in point
and
← thru the leg loops

Common Uses
• Securing nut cordage
• Backup knot for most others

Secondary Use
• Joining two ropes

Half of a Double Fisherman's tied into the tail of a Figure Eight Follow-Through as a backup.

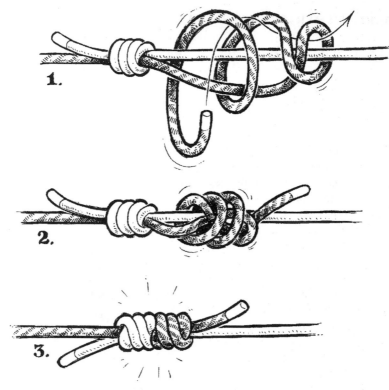

Triple Fisherman's Knot.

TRIPLE FISHERMAN'S

Certain cordage, such as Spectra or Kevlar, is quite slick and stiff. Consequently, knots have a difficult time keeping their wraps. The Triple Fisherman's is a relatively new knot designed to keep a good hold in such cords. It is identical to the Double Fisherman's, except that the ropes are wrapped three times around each other.

Common Use
• Joining slick, stiff Spectra and Kevlar cordage

FIGURE EIGHT

The Figure Eight, also known as a Flemish Knot, enjoys the same general use as the Overhand—that of a stopper knot. Tie it in the end of rappel or belay ropes to prevent tragedy. The Figure Eight is slightly harder to tie than the Overhand and takes more rope, but it's bulkier—a desirable characteristic for a stopper knot—less likely to untie itself, and easier to untie after it has been drawn tight.

Common Uses
- Stopper knot in the end of a belay rope
- Stopper knot in the end of a rappel rope

Figure Eight.

1.　　　　**2.**　　　　**3.**

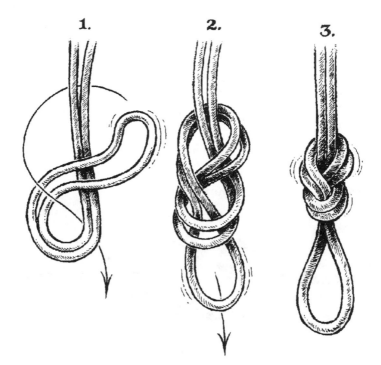

Figure Eight on a Bight.

FIGURE EIGHT ON A BIGHT

This is one of the most necessary and functional knots. You could learn to climb knowing only two knots, the Figure Eight on a Bight and the Figure Eight Follow-Through. The Figure Eight Follow-Through would join you to rope, and the Figure Eight on a Bight would join your rope to the anchors. For this latter use, the knot is without peers. It is strong, simple, and not apt to slip. The only disadvantage to the Figure Eight on a Bight is that it's not easy to adjust. Until you develop a feel for how much rope the knot consumes versus the distance to your anchor, you're likely to end up with a system that's either too tight or too slack.

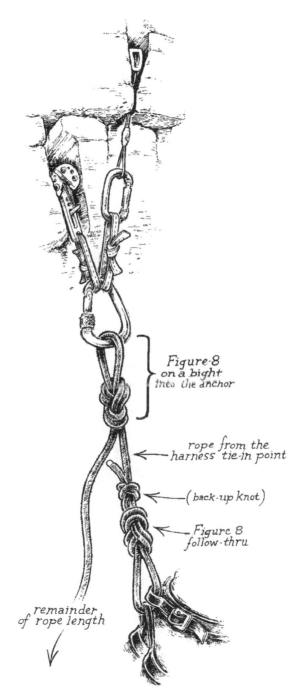

Figure·8
on a bight
into the anchor

rope from the
harness tie·in point

(back·up knot)

Figure·8
follow·thru

remainder
of rope length

**The Figure-8 on a Bight is the best knot
to use when connecting a rope to an anchor.**

Besides being the premier anchor knot, the Figure Eight on a Bight makes a passable middleman's knot (clip to it with two carabiners having their gates opposed and reversed or, better, use locking carabiners), although the Butterfly is better, being easier to untie after it has held a hard load. Likewise, you can use the Figure Eight on a Bight to tie out a short section of rope that has been damaged; just don't expect the knot to slide through any carabiners.

Tie the Figure Eight on a Bight near the end of a rope, and you can use it to clip a haul line to your harness.

Common Uses
- Anchoring rope to protection
- Attaching middleman for glacier travel
- Attaching haul line to harness

Secondary Use
- Tying out a damaged section of rope

A damaged section of rope tied-out using the Figure Eight on a Bight.

FIGURE EIGHT FISHERMAN'S

This knot is really a Figure Eight Bend, but as you can tie this bend two different ways, for clarity I'm calling this version the Fisherman's, which I've seen it called elsewhere.

I find great comfort in this knot, knowing that it absolutely will not come untied when used to join two rappel ropes. It's also the most secure knot for tying together two top ropes. In both uses, leave a long tail on each end, and tie this off with a Double Fisherman's Backup.

A minor disadvantage of the Figure Eight Fisherman's is that it gobbles up a hearty length of rope. A major disadvantage is that it's bulky and likes to jam in fissures, behind flakes, and so on when you pull it down the cliff.

Common Uses
• Tying top ropes together
• Tying rappel ropes together

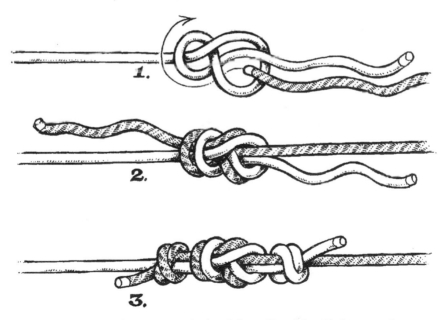

Figure Eight Fisherman's tied with a Double Fisherman's as a backup.

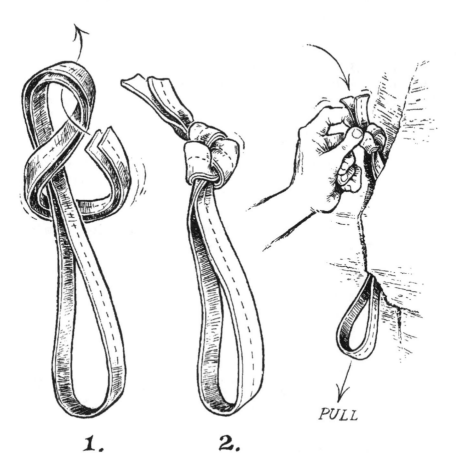

1.　　　**2.**

A jammed Figure Eight Loop.

FIGURE EIGHT LOOP

The only use I've ever found for the Figure Eight Loop was as jammed-knot protection, and I didn't really find this—the Saxon sandstone legend Bernt Arnold showed it to me. As jammed-knot protection, the Figure Eight Loop presents a slightly different profile than the Overhand Loop and so has value on your knot rack. To use, follow the prescription given for jamming the Overhand Loop. You can tie this knot in webbing, rope, or cord.

Common Use
• None

Secondary Use
• Improvised jammed-knot protection

FIGURE EIGHT FOLLOW-THROUGH

The most critical knot for the climber is the one that joins the rope to the harness. If this knot is tied incorrectly, or the wrong knot is used, all is lost. The failure of the tie-in knot, or that of the climber to tie in properly to begin with, ranks with anchor failure and rappeling off the end of the rope as a leading cause of death and injury.

Because your tie-in knot carries such a heavy burden, it must be infallible and easy to tie in all situations. The Figure Eight Follow-Through fills both orders. It's also easy to learn yet difficult to forget, and it yields to visual inspection—this knot looks either right or wrong. That it is difficult to untie this knot after it has held a high load is the only disadvantage to this knot, and that is a small one considering the peace of mind it provides. Those of you who fall frequently and hard, however, should try the Double Bowline with Jack's Variation. It's equally reliable although more confusing to tie, but it's easy to untie after holding a fall.

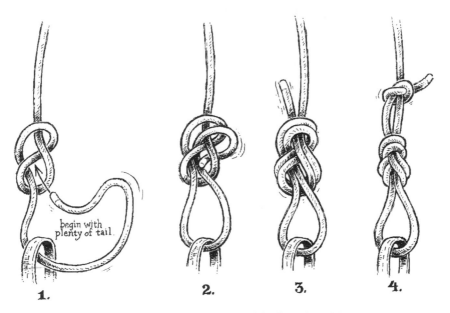

begin with plenty of tail.

1.   2.   3.   4.

Figure Eight Follow-Through with Overhand backup.

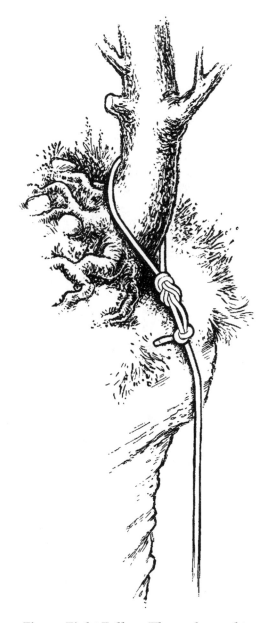

A final and equally important use for the Figure Eight Follow-Through is for tying the rope around trees, horns, boulders, and other loopable protuberances. In this capacity, the knot is again without equal.

When you tie the Figure Eight Follow-Through, make certain you leave a long tail, and finish this with a Double Fisherman's.

Common Uses
• Connecting rope to climbing harness
• Tying rope around trees, boulders, and so on

Figure Eight Follow-Through, used to secure rope to tree.

Bowline
(with a single loop)

The Single Bowline is simple, but can easily be tied incorrectly.

SINGLE BOWLINE

If you know nothing about knots, you still likely have heard the Bowline ditty: The rabbit comes out of the hole, goes around the tree, then goes back in the hole.

One of the original sailing knots, the Bowline immediately found its way among landlubbing climbers, who savored its strength and the ease with which it unties after holding a load. Unfortunately, the Single Bowline is a traitorous knot and likes to untie itself in moments of need. For that reason, the Single Bowline is *not recommended for climbing*, other than to attach a cord to a nut tool. I include it here only because you must know how to tie the Single Bowline to master the Double Bowline.

Common Use
• Attaching keeper cord to a nut tool

DOUBLE BOWLINE WITH JACK'S VARIATION

The Single Bowline has left such a foul taste with so many people that the bitterness has worn off on its cousin, the Double Bowline. Indeed, many climbers are afraid of the Double Bowline. For many years, I counted myself among them and wouldn't touch the Double Bowline.

Then a good friend, Jack Mileski, showed me a clever way to tuck the tail back out the hole and rest it against the tree. His extra step keeps pressure on the tail, locking it. Add a Double Grapevine to the end as a final safety, and you have a knot you can trust. What's more, the knot is still easy to untie, even after it's held a heavy person.

Like the Figure Eight Follow-Through, you can use the Double Bowline to anchor the rope around a tree or boulder. Since, however, this practice often requires that you tie the knot from an unusual perspective (below or underneath the knot, for example), I have a hard time endorsing it. Before you use the Double Bowline, make sure you are expert in its use and able to recognize when it's tied incorrectly. Tie the Bowline wrong (a common mistake is to put the rabbit in the hole first, instead of having it come out of the hole), and it can still appear correct to a cloudy mind but fall apart as soon as it's weighted.

Common Uses
• Joining rope to harness
• Tying rope around trees, boulders, and so on

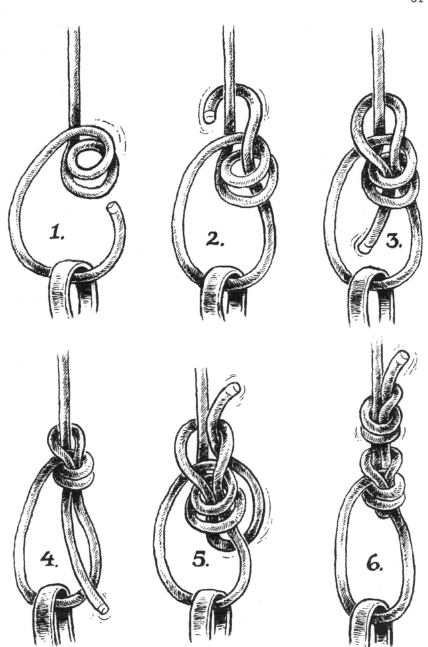

Double Bowline with Jack's Variation, using a Double Fisherman's to secure the tail.

1.
Begin
with
(at least)
four snug
wraps

BOWLINE ON A COIL

Another old nautical knot, the Bowline on a Coil, was, I suspect, the keel-haul knot of choice. Climbers will find it equally gruesome. This knot, used as an emergency harness, can choke you if you hang in it for long. Still, it's a valuable knot, just in case. Four wraps around the waist is the norm, but if rope is short, two or three wraps work almost as well. As with all tie-in knots, secure the Bowline on a Coil with a Double Fisherman's, tied around the waist loops. If you need to hang on the rope for long, make

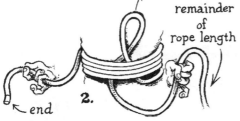

remainder
of
rope length

← end

2.

5.

3.

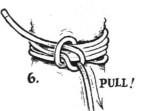

6. PULL!

Lock·off!

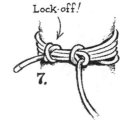

4.

7.

Bowline on Coil.

one of your initial waist wraps loose, and slip it under your butt to form a seat that will take some of the load off your waist. Watch that you tie this knot correctly; done wrong—without locking off all the waist loops—it can become a slip noose and kill you.

Common Use
• None

Secondary Use
• Improvised harness

Butterfly Knot (page 34) used by a middleman.

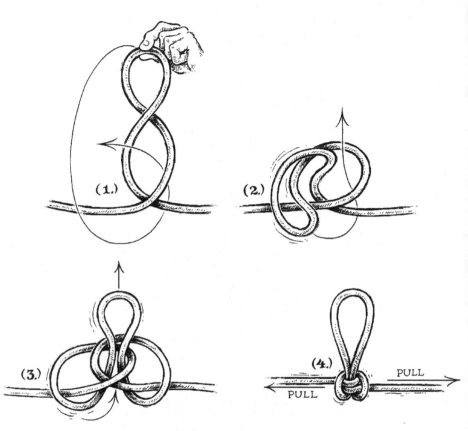

Butterfly Knot.

BUTTERFLY KNOT

Like canned food and satellite TV, this knot originated in war, where it was used to join man to rope so he could drag cannons through bogs. In peacetime, this Butterfly Knot, or Lineman's Loop, is useful to the climber wishing to anchor himself to the middle of the rope, a common practice in glacier travel. To do so, clip yourself to the knot with two carabiners that have their gates reversed and opposed. In the ideal scenario, one of the carabiners will be locking. You may also use this knot to tie out a damaged section of rope; just know that the knot won't slide through your protection or rappel device.

Common Uses
• Middleman's tie-in knot
• Tying out damaged section of rope

SQUARE FISHERMAN'S

The maxim of rope strength states that the strength of a knot depends on the ease of its curves. In simpler terms, all this really means is that knots with sharp turns are weaker than those that make gradual bends. That said, the Square Knot, which bends a sharp 45 degrees not once but four times, is about the weakest knot you can tie. I've heard that the Square Knot retains only 45 percent of a rope's strength, whereas other knots such as the Double Bowline retain 75 percent. Besides being hopelessly weak, the Square Knot is also easy to tie wrong. Reverse one of the crossing passes, and the knot will hold just long enough to get you into trouble—or killed.

You would think, then, that the Square Knot's crippling flaws would preclude it from climbing. They do, but a variation, the Square Fisherman's, works well to join two rappel lines. Used for this purpose, the knot is easy to untie when you're finished, and it's safe provided you leave long tails and anchor these with a Double Fisherman's backup. *Do not use the Square Knot without the backup knots.*

Common Use
• Joining rappel ropes

Square Knot with backup.

HALF HITCH

By itself, the Half Hitch is near worthless. Its only use is as a backup, to secure the end of more trustworthy knots. Even then, you should employ the Half Hitch only when no other backup will do, such as when you are out of rope and the miserly Half Hitch is the only knot that will fit in the short piece.

Common Use
• None

Secondary Use
• Inadequate backup for other knots

Half Hitch.

DOUBLE HALF HITCH

The Double Half Hitch is two Half Hitches tied one after the other, and is a popular knot for securing tent guylines. Despite the name, it's not twice as good as the single Half Hitch. In fact, there is no good use for this knot; if you have enough rope to tie it, you also have enough rope (and wherewithal) to tie the better Double Fisherman's. The Double Half Hitch is included here only so that you know what it is and to avoid it.

Common Use
• Securing tent line

Secondary Use
• None

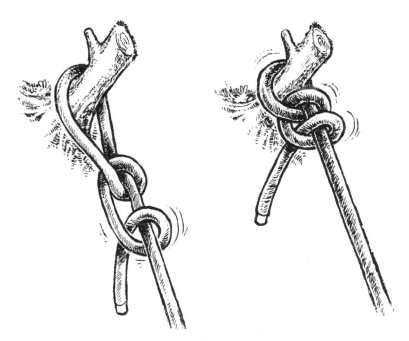

Double Half Hitch.

RING BEND

The Ring Bend has a mind of its own. And a devious one at that. Turn your back on it and it will loosen itself and come undone. Despite its poor character, the Ring Bend is a favorite for tying webbing, as it has the redeeming qualities of being simple, clean, and easy to visually inspect. Use this knot to fashion runners and tie-offs from webbing; be sure to leave a 3-inch tail on each side of the knot.

On occasion I've seen climbers use the Ring Bend to join their top ropes or rappel lines. I recommend against this; the Figure Eight Bend and Double Fisherman's are safer.

Common Use

• Tying webbing into loops

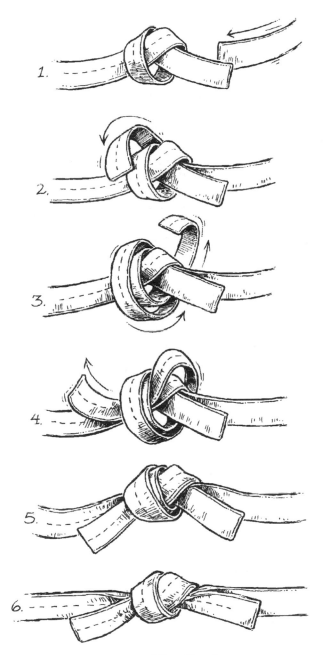

Tying a Ring Bend.

CLOVE HITCH

In the days of the tall-masted ships, the Clove Hitch made the ratlines (rope ladders) fast to the shrouds. On mountains, the Clove Hitch fastens rope to anchor. It's advantageous for this chore, as it's the only anchor knot that you can readily adjust and so get the anchors closer to equalized.

The drawbacks to the Clove Hitch are that it can slip, loosen, and creep up the carabiner and open its gate. Used improperly, or if it is allowed to go unsupervised, the knot is exceedingly dangerous. Do not use it in situations where it's the lone anchor knot. (I use the Clove Hitch as a secondary knot to back up anchors tied in with the Figure Eight on a Bight.) And do not tie it in the end of a rope, lest it slip and the tail pull through.

When you do use the Clove Hitch, arrange it so the loaded strand is next to the carabiner's spine. Go the other way and the knot will load the carabiner's gate side, which is far weaker than the spine. Ideally, you would always use a locking carabiner with the Clove Hitch. Before you trust yourself to the Clove Hitch, pull both of its ends as hard as you can to set the knot.

A final use for the Clove Hitch will interest the aid climber who needs to tie off a partly driven piton or a bolt missing its hanger. For this use, tie the Clove Hitch in a webbing tie-off loop, slip the loop over the piton or bolt so its loaded strand will be against the rock, and cinch up.

Common Uses
• Joining rope to anchors
• Tying off protruding pitons, bolts, and ice screws

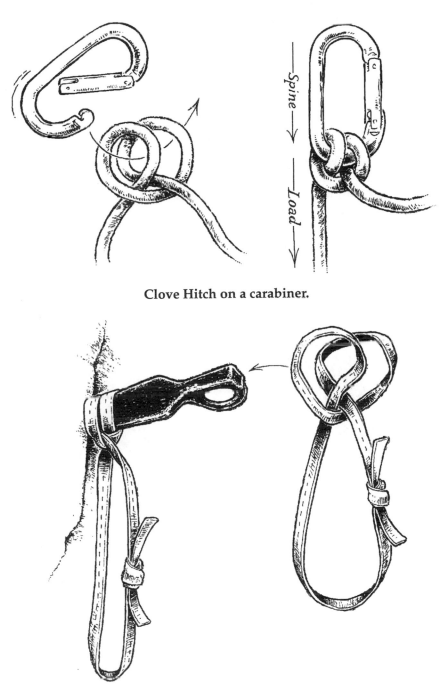

Clove Hitch on a carabiner.

Clove Hitch on a piton.

SLIP KNOT

The Slip Knot is a noose knot, and it's also technically a hitch. It's used like the Girth Hitch to tie off pitons and ice screws that haven't driven their full distance. Unlike the Girth Hitch, though, the Slip Knot is of one mind and doesn't enjoy other uses. Still, it's the aid climber's friend, easy to tie with one hand, and equally easy to untie. When you use the Slip Knot, cinch it up snug and clip it so that the weight-bearing strand continues to pull the knot tighter; take care not to reverse this, or the knot will loosen and fall off. The Slip Knot is especially useful for cinching over protruding pitons, ice screws, and bolts, as it's the trimmest tie-off knot and places the load closer to the rock than the Girth Hitch or Clove Hitch.

Common Use
• Tying off protruding pitons, ice screws, and bolts

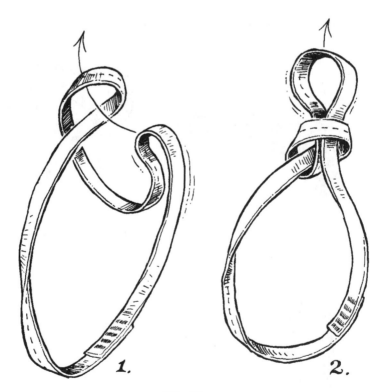

Slip Knot.

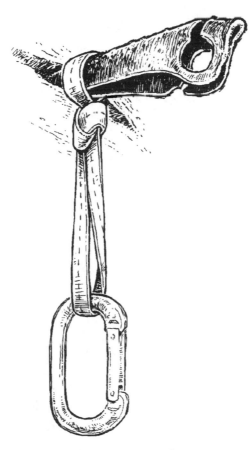

Slip Knot on a piton.

GIRTH HITCH

The Girth Hitch is as useful as it's simple. Hitch a sling or runner through your harness, and you create a "daisy chain" or clip-in loop. Girth Hitch a sling around a tree or jammed chockstone, and you have an anchor ready to clip.

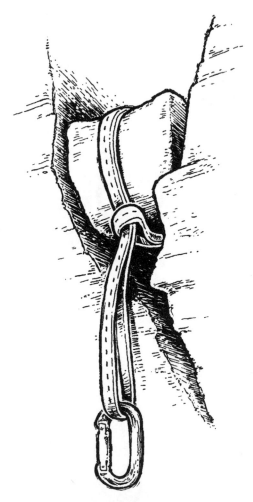

Runner girthed to a harness.

Common Uses
• Attaching a daisy chain to harness
• Tying off trees, jammed rocks, or horns
• Tying off protruding pitons and ice screws
• Attaching a sling to water-jug handle

Runner girthed to a chockstone.

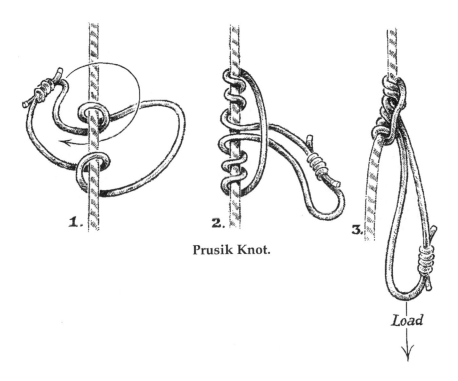

Prusik Knot.

Load

PRUSIK

Before a Swiss bird scientist invented mechanical ascenders in the 1960s, climbers used the Prusik Knot to ascend fixed ropes. This variation on the Girth Hitch grips the rope like a clenched fist when you weight it. Unweight the knot, and you can easily slide it up the rope. Use two Prusiks and you can alternate weighting and unweighting and shimmy up a rope. On the first ascent of El Capitan's Nose in 1958, Warren Harding and team fixed 2,000 feet of rope and prusiked all of it.

Today, the Prusik still has its uses, and in certain situations it's the best tool for the job. It's, for example, the safest way to ape across a horizontally or diagonally strung rope, where mechanical ascenders can torque and pop off. Also, the Prusik is a common rappel backup and is a godsend in emergency situations, such as when you fall below an overhang and are unable to get back on the rock. In such cases, you can fashion Prusiks from most any sling, cord, even shoestring (thinking climbers carry a couple Prusik loops on their racks to handle such situations) and simply climb up the rope.

The best Prusik is made from durable, 5- or 6-millimeter perlon cord tied in 1-foot loops and secured with a Double Fisherman's. Three to four wraps around the rope will usually give the best hold. Add wraps if the knot slips. In a pinch, I've made Prusiks from almost anything, from 1-inch webbing to 9-millimeter rope. All work to some degree, but you do have to experiment with the number of wraps to make the Prusik grip properly. When you are prusiking double ropes, wrap both Prusiks around both ropes rather than put one Prusik on each rope.

Regardless of what material you use for the Prusik, dress it evenly, weight it slowly, and loosen it well before you slide it up the rope. All Prusiks have a finite life and will eventually burn through (small cord is less durable than the fat stuff), so inspect them regularly.

If you use the Prusik to back up a rappel, make sure the sling that attaches the Prusik to the harness is short and always within easy reach. At least one climber has died because his sling was too long and locked up out of reach, stranding him on rappel.

Rappel with a Prusik as a backup.

Common Uses
• Ascending single or double rope
• Rappeling backup

Secondary Uses
• Tying off belay
• Improvising hauling system

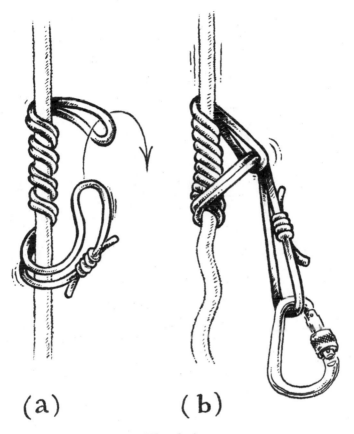

(a) **(b)**

Klemheist.

KLEMHEIST

When you wrap a loop of cord around the rope, you get the Klemheist. This variation on the Prusik works similarly but is easier to slide up the rope and thus is the preferred knot for lengthy ascents. Add more wraps to generate more friction, as you do with the Prusik. Unlike the Prusik, the Klemheist grips best when you load it straight down. When you have a diagonal or horizontal rope to cross, the Prusik is the safer knot. You can tie a Klemheist in webbing as well as cord, but webbing generally doesn't grip as well.

Common Use
• Ascending single and double rope

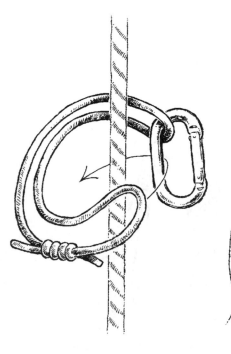

Bachman on a single rope.

Load

Bachman on a double rope.

Load

BACHMAN

Weave the Klemheist around a carabiner, and you get the Bachman. Before I had Jumars (mechanical ascenders), this was my favorite knot for climbing fixed ropes. It slides up the rope with less effort than the Klemheist and is much easier to loosen. Don't, however, mistake the carabiner for a handle; grab the carabiner, either by accident or on purpose, and the knot will slide down the rope. As with the Klemheist, don't use the Bachman to cross a traversing rope. The Bachman is the best ascending knot for double ropes. For best performance, place the carabiner between the two lines.

Common Use
• Ascending single and double rope

AUTOBLOCK

This knot is fast becoming the ascending and holding knot of choice among rescuers, because it's relatively easy to release when it's loaded. Tie the Autoblock with cord or webbing.

Common Use
• Ascending or holding rope

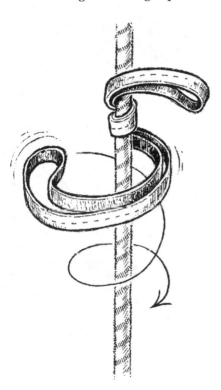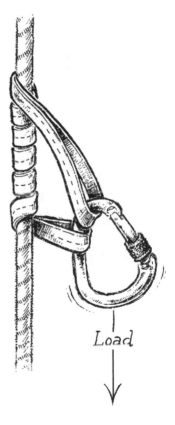

Load

Autoblock.

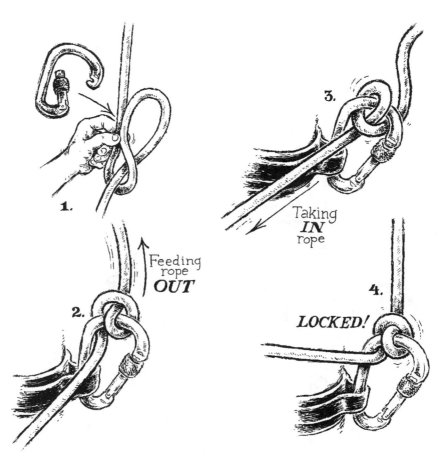

Munter Hitch.

MUNTER HITCH

It's inevitable that at some point in your climbing career you will be on a cliff or mountain in sore need of a belay or rappel device. In these situations, you'll praise the Munter Hitch. This sliding knot provides sufficient friction for either belaying or rappeling and works on single or double ropes down to about 8 millimeter. The Munter Hitch works so well, in fact, that the UIAA has adopted it as a valid belay, and numerous climbers have discarded their belay devices and rely entirely on the Munter Hitch.

As useful as the Munter Hitch is, it also has a bad habit of twisting and tangling your rope. This is why the Munter Hitch is a vital knot to know for emergencies but a poor one for regular use.

You can rig the Munter Hitch on most any carabiner, but because the knot is large and needs to swivel, it works best on a large HMS Pearabiner. Because your life depends on the knot, also be sure to use a locking carabiner. If you are double-rope rappeling, you can either tie both ropes into one Munter Hitch and clip them to one carabiner, or tie them independently and give each one its own carabiner. I prefer the second method, as it doesn't twist the ropes as badly.

Finally, when you use the Munter Hitch in belay mode, arrange it so the loaded side of the knot is against the carabiner's spine. Reversing this setup will cause the weaker gate side of the carabiner to be loaded.

Common Uses
- Belay knot
- Rappel knot

CARABINER WRAP

The Carabiner Wrap looks dubious but is nevertheless useful to climbers. This simple method of wrapping the rope around a carabiner's spine lets you rappel a single rope of most any diameter. I've even used it to rappel 7-millimeter cord. Adding to its beauty in dire situations, the Carabiner Wrap requires only one carabiner.

The Carabiner Wrap doesn't need much explaining, and common sense will tell you that you can add wraps to increase friction or remove wraps to decrease friction. Make sure the wraps go on the carabiner's solid spine, use a locking carabiner if available, and don't let the knot twist up into itself or invert.

Common Use
- Emergency rappel

Carabiner Wrap.

MULE KNOT

The Mule Knot is a friction knot that you can release while it's under load, although it can take some fiddling to do so. It's one of those special knots you'll rarely use but will praise when you do.

Use the Mule Knot to tie off your belay device and free your hands, as you'll need to do when the leader has fallen and is injured, and you need both hands to facilitate a rescue. In everyday situations, you can use the Mule Knot to temporarily tie off the belay and pass up gear to the leader, eat, tend to calls of nature, and so on. In all situations, clip a carabiner through the Mule Knot to prevent it from accidentally slipping. If you don't have a carabiner, use the standing portion of the Mule Knot to tie an Overhand backup around the active (loaded) side of the rope. Also, don't forget to pass the initial loop of the Mule Knot through your belay carabiner.

To release the Mule Knot, unclip the backup carabiner or untie the backup Overhand, and pull on the standing (unloaded) side of the knot.

Common Use
• Tying off lead rope to free your hands

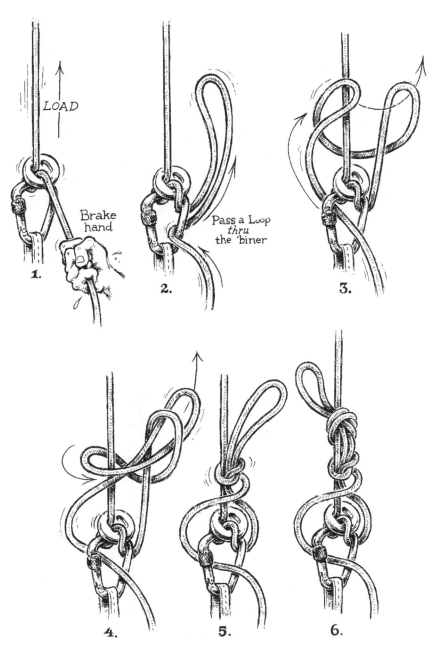

Mule Knot.

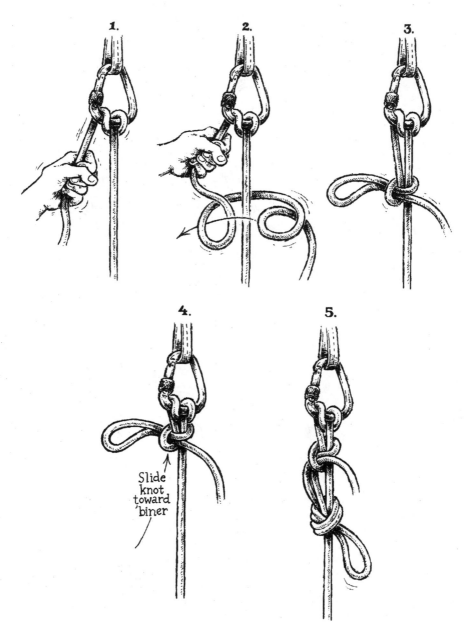

1.

2.

3.

4.

Slide
knot
toward
'biner

5.

Munter Mule.

MUNTER MULE
If you're belaying or rappeling with the Munter Hitch, you'll need the Munter Mule if you are to tie off the rope and free your hands. The Munter Mule is simply a Mule Knot tied on the standing side of a Munter Hitch. Before you tie the Munter Mule, be sure the rope is taut; a slack rope can cause you to orient the knot in the wrong direction. Tie the Munter Mule around the active (loaded) side of the rope, and *do not* pass a bight of rope through the belay/rappel carabiner before tying the Munter Mule. Clip a carabiner through the Munter Mule's open loop to prevent it from slipping, or use the Overhand backup as discussed with the Mule Knot.

Common Use
• Tying off lead or rappel rope to free your hands

MARINER KNOT
The Mariner Knot, illustrated on page 56, is a complex, exotic knot that, like the Mule Knot and Munter Mule, is releasable when under load. Unlike the Mule and Munter Mule, however, you do not tie the Mariner Knot in the lead or rappel rope. Rather, you take a loop of $\%_{6}$-inch webbing and wind this around a carabiner, and then around the loop itself. The common use of the Mariner Knot is to transfer the load from your belay device to an independent anchor. The Mariner Knot loosens and slips when it isn't weighted; keep an eye on it.

Common Use
• Transferring weight from one anchor to another

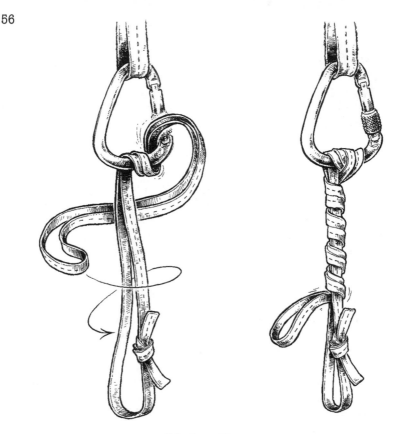

Mariner Knot.

GARDA HART KNOT

As sure as you'll wind up on a climb without a belay device, you'll also end up without a pulley but needing to haul a heavy pack or assist a struggling partner up a pitch. The Garda Hart, a one-directional sliding knot, is tailor-made for the situation. To rig, clip two similar carabiners (two ovals, for example) to a sling that runs through your belay anchor. Clip and weave the rope through the carabiners as shown. Be careful to orient the carabiner gates so that they open on top. To use, pull on the unweighted side of the rope and voilà—the pack, or your friend, rises. (If you've threaded the rope wrong, it will be able to slide in both directions; test before you commit.) Relax your grip, and the carabiners pin the rope, letting you

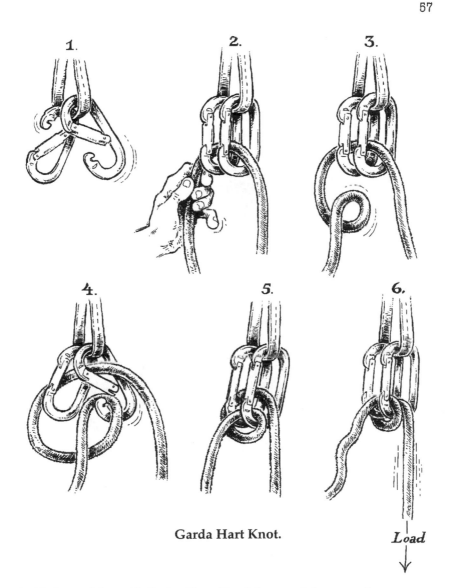

Garda Hart Knot.

Load

hold the weight with little effort. Don't let go of the rope, however, as the Garda Hart can slip. Watch that the knot doesn't creep up onto the carabiner gates and unclip itself.

Common Uses
• Emergency pack hauling
• Assisting a partner up a pitch

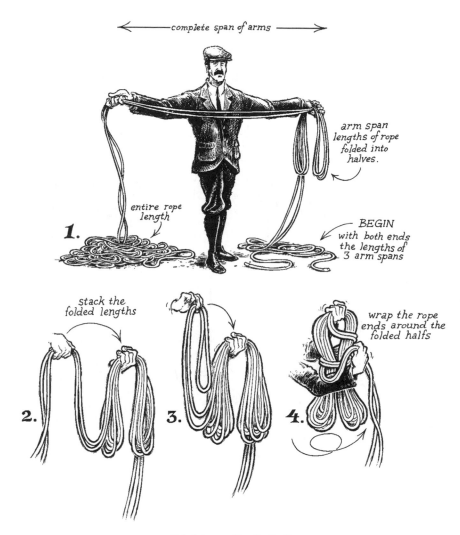

←——— *complete span of arms* ———→

arm span lengths of rope folded into halves.

entire rope length

1.

BEGIN with both ends the lengths of 3 arm spans

stack the folded lengths

2.

3.

4.

wrap the rope ends around the folded halfs

Making a Pack Coil.

PACK COIL

The Pack Coil looks shabby, but it's the simplest, quickest, and least twist-inducing method of coiling the rope. Start with both ends in one hand, heave three to four arm spans of rope onto the ground, then begin collecting the rest in the palm of one hand. When you're done, you can carry the rope on your back, pack-style, using the ends of the rope as two handy shoulder straps and wrapping them around your trunk. Finish the "waist belt" with a Square Knot.

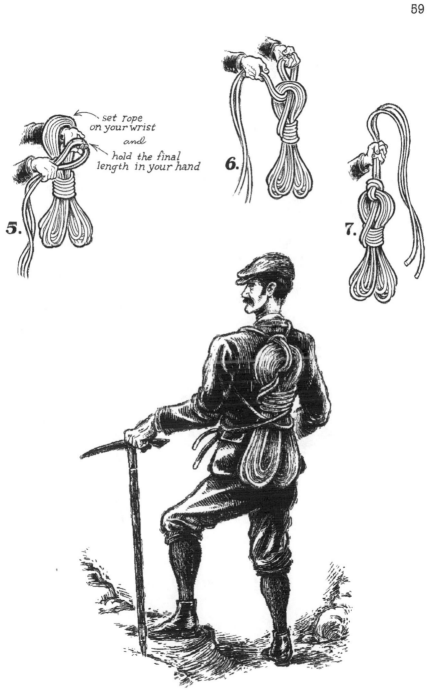

set rope
on your wrist
and
hold the final
length in your hand

5.

6.

7.

The Pack Coil.

LAP COIL

If you prefer nice-looking, even coils for picture taking or posing, the Lap Coil is your method. Otherwise, it's hateful and induces countless kinks and twists into the rope. You can lead entire pitches in the time it takes to unfurl a line that has been coiled with the Lap method. It does, however, have the redeeming quality that you get to sit while you coil.

Making a Lap Coil.

The Lap Coil.

5

On Rope

My first climbing rope was a moldy nylon hank of cord my buddy Donnie found tied to a boat out at Crowder Lake. We were only thirteen years old and figured, what the hey, a rope was a rope, and a free rope let you save your money for bicycle tires and jerky. We made harnesses from pack lash straps, used nails for pitons and tiny 29-cent rapid links for carabiners, and went climbing and rappeling. The luck of youth was on our side, for neither of us ever took a serious tumble. Perhaps our rudimentary equipment was just inadequate enough to keep us from getting into real difficulties. A couple years later, I got an REI catalog and ordered what I thought was a proper climbing rope, a twisted Goldline. Again, we were lucky. Goldline, while strong enough to hold a fall, stretches like a bungee cord. Take a hard fall on a Goldline, and rope stretch is likely to drop you on a ledge or the ground.

By the time we turned sixteen and got our drivers' licenses we had come to a realization: There's only one type of rope acceptable for climbing—the *kernmantle* rope. Kernmantle rope is a two-piece rope made of nylon. It has a braided outer sheath, the *mantle*, and braided or twisted inner strands, the core or *kern*. Most of the rope's strength comes from the core. The mantle

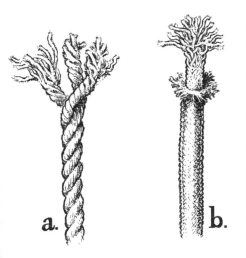

a. A twisted rope.
b. A kernmantle rope.

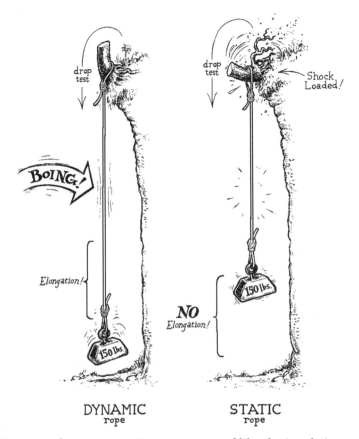

DYNAMIC
rope

STATIC
rope

functions mostly as a protective cover, sort of like the insulation over an extension cord.

Kernmantle ropes have many applications beyond climbing. Firemen, spelunkers, roofers, roughnecks, criminals, and other people use them every day for working in high places. The ropes they use look much like climbing ropes but in fact are radically different. Their ropes are *static*, like steel cable. Fall on a static rope, and the sudden jolt of being caught is enough to snap your neck.

Climbing ropes are *dynamic*. They are woven and braided so that they can absorb much of the force of a fall without unduly stretching like my old Goldline or a rubber band. The dynamic property of a climbing rope sets it apart. All other ropes are unfit for climbing.

How do you know if you have a climbing rope? Climbing ropes look distinctly different, having multicolored sheaths. Static ropes are typically a solid color, usually white or black, with maybe one band of contrasting piping. More telling, all climbing ropes will be certified by the Union Internationale des Association d'Alpinisme. The UIAA is an international body that sets guidelines for climbing ropes and equipment. Ropes approved by the UIAA will not break in normal situations. Reputable climbing shops will sell only UIAA-stamped ropes, but some frauds do make it to market. Check before you buy. A UIAA-approved rope will state so on its hangtag, and there will be a UIAA logo taped to both ends of the rope.

ROPE DIAMETERS

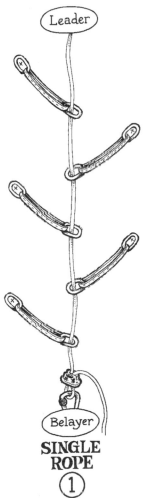

Single ropes are those designated by the UIAA as safe for single-strand use. This is the sort of rope that rock and big-wall climbers find the most suitable, largely because it is the simplest rope to manage and is the lightest in weight. Single ropes come in diameters from 9.8 to 11 millimeters. Sport climbers, to whom every ounce is the enemy, typically use 9.8- to 10-millimeter ropes, since these are the lightest. That these skinny ropes also wear out quicker than fatter ropes is of minor concern to people to whom performance is everything. Traditional and big-wall climbers often opt for the thicker, more durable 10- and 11-millimeter ropes. Thick ropes are also a wise choice for beginners, who are notoriously hard on their ropes, and for sport climbers who want a sturdy "work" rope. All single ropes have the number 1, surrounded by a circle, on the rope's whipped ends.

Double ropes are those that you must use in pairs, although you don't need to clip every rope through every point of protection. Rather, you can alternate clipping the ropes, an appreciated feature that reduces rope on winding and traversing routes. You'll find double ropes in the 8- to 9-mil-

Leader

Belayer

SINGLE ROPE

①

limeter range. Double ropes are ideal for ice, alpine, and mountaineering, where you typically need two ropes to rappel the route and carrying two heavy single ropes doesn't make sense. Double ropes are also popular for climbs with loose or sharp rock, where the risk of cutting a rope is high. All double ropes have the number ½, surrounded by a circle, on the rope's whipped ends.

Twin ropes are the most dysfunctional of the lot, and I've never been able to rationalize a place for them. These 7- to 9-millimeter lines are used in pairs like double ropes but differ drastically, as both strands must be clipped to every point of protection. In my eyes, clipping both ropes robs them of the great advantage of double ropes—that of alternating clips to minimize rope drag. Also, these small-diameter ropes are snag and tangle prone, and I can never seem to keep them orderly. Still, twin ropes provide the highest safety margin of all ropes and are the lightest combination possible, making them appealing to a few extreme alpinists. The rest of us will never have use for them. Twin ropes have the number 2, surrounded by a circle, on the rope's whipping. Don't confuse twin ropes with double ropes; they are similar but not interchangeable.

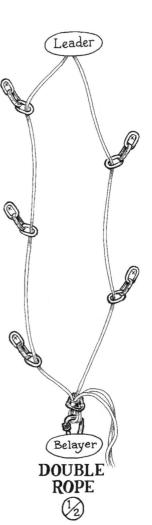

DOUBLE ROPE

ROPE LENGTHS

Inflation has gotten hold of ropes. Twenty years ago you bought either a 120-foot rope or a 150-foot rope. Today you must choose among 165 (50-meter), 181 (55-meter), 198 (60-meter), and even 330-foot (100-meter) lengths. (You can still buy a few ropes in archaic 150-foot lengths; this length saves you a couple dollars but isn't practical or recommended.) I'm not sure why ropes have grown longer, other than it makes sense: better to have too much rope, and be guaranteed that ledge or anchor high up, than to have too little and come up short and

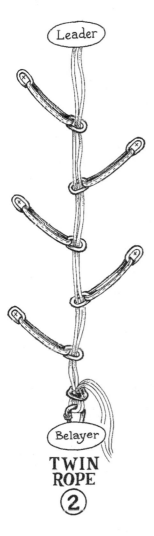

Leader

Belayer

TWIN ROPE
②

uncomfortable.

Fifty-meter ropes are what most of us use. These are adequate for most single-pitch traditional routes. Longer, 55-meter ropes are popular with big-wall, ice, and sport climbers for a variety of reasons. Primarily, numerous new routes are established with 55-meter ropes. Shorter ropes just don't reach the belay or lowering anchors. Fifty-five-meter ropes are also more efficient, as they let you skip belay stations and run pitches together, eliminating belay change-over, saving time. If the descent requires rappeling, 55-meter ropes get down in fewer rappels. And as ropes frequently wear the worst near the ends, when the ends of a 55-meter rope wear out, you can trim them off and still have a functional 50-meter rope. Keep in mind, however, that trimming the ends doesn't mean you have a new rope—the middle section you're still using has already held a number of falls.

Ropes longer than 55-meters are too specialized for the recreational or even fairly serious climber. Sixty-meter ropes are mostly used for speed climbing, where, again, running pitches together lets you save time. One-hundred-meter ropes are always double 9-millimeter or thinner and are bicolored; at 50 meters, the rope has a distinct pattern or color change. This rope's gangly length is often necessary to stretch between ledges or good belays on extreme alpine routes and eliminates the need for a joining knot, a comfortable asset when you pull down the rappel ropes.

ROPE TREATMENTS
Many ropes are treated with a water-repellent coating. The "dry" treatment adds a few dollars to the rope but also improves rope performance and durability and helps keep the rope dry. I never buy an

untreated rope.

The least expensive treatment is a topical job, usually a sort of paraffin, sprayed or otherwise applied to the sheath only. It's better than nothing, but once it wears off—on your hands much of the time—the rest of the rope is defenseless against water.

The best treatments are applied to the individual yarns in the core and sheath during manufacturing. This process yields the most durable and effective treatment. The bad news is that the manufacturers often don't tell you what treatment method they've used, or distort the facts into incomprehensible gibberish. About the only way to know for sure is to try the rope yourself, until you get one you're satisfied with.

Mountaineers, ice climbers, and big-wall climbers who can get caught high up in storms can appreciate how a dry-treated rope doesn't sponge up water, but if you only climb rock and only do so when it's dry, do you need a treated rope? Yes. Dry treatments do more than keep water absorption to a minimum. They also make the rope softer and smoother, which makes it easier to manage and knot, and it will glide over the rock with less friction than a stiff, untreated rope.

ROPE TESTING

Many myths surround the UIAA, rope testing, and ropes. The most prevalent is that ropes with a higher *number of falls held* are superior to ones with fewer. Some misguided people hold falls held as the ultimate benchmark for rope quality and buy based solely on this deceiving number. Before we go into why such claims are mostly rubbish, you should understand how the UIAA drop test works. With single and twin ropes, a 176-pound weight is dropped approximately 16 feet on 9 feet of rope that is tied off to the scaffolding. The test sounds tame, but it's a bit like a hanging and is an eye opener when you see it. The snap on the rope is appalling. You need witness only one such drop to reaffirm your faith in climbing ropes. The test is so severe that it's nearly impossible to duplicate in real life, where the give in the belay, your body, the runners on protection, your knots cinching up, the friction of your body grating down the face, slippage through the belay device, and all the other uncounted and often unknown factors keep the impact forces well below those generated in the lab. And the UIAA requires that single and double ropes withstand five such drops.

Twin ropes must survive twelve test falls.

The strenuousness of the UIAA test assures that any passing rope is safe. Ropes that go beyond the minimum requirements aren't necessarily stronger or safer or longer wearing. About all you know for certain is that they can survive a good number of test drops and cost more. And, unknown to most customers, the number of falls held as stated on the rope's hangtag is supplied by the manufacturer, not the UIAA. A shady manufacturer can, for example, list a rope as an eight-fall though only one sample held that number of test drops. The other samples might have held only six or seven. Meanwhile, another manufacturer could get the same results but list its rope as a six-fall. As a consumer, you have no way of knowing who is conservative and who stretches the envelope. All you see are the numbers six and eight. The UIAA doesn't care one way or another so long as the samples sustained five drops.

A more telling number than falls held is the *maximum impact force.* This indicates how much force a rope is able to absorb. Since you and your protection feel the brunt of the impact force, the lower this number, the better you two will be. The UIAA lists the maximum impact force at 2,640 pounds for single and twin ropes and 1,760 for double ropes. They do, however, allow ropes to stretch 45 percent of their length to absorb the force and do not require the manufacturer to list dynamic elongation. Thus, it is possible to purchase a low-impact-force rope that will, to your dismay, stretch like a Slinky when you drop onto it.

Oddly, the UIAA does require that a rope's *static elongation* be noted on the hangtag. Static elongation is the amount a rope will stretch when you hang on it, as you do to rappel, jumar, or lower. The exact test loads 3 feet of rope with 176 pounds. If a single rope stretches less than 8 percent and a double rope less than 10 percent, they get the seal of approval. Nice, but meaningless.

All this mumbo jumbo means is that you must evaluate every aspect to get a rope that's a proper fit for you. Consider diameter, length, dry treatment, falls held, and maximum impact force against cost, how you will use the rope, and how often. Get all the pieces to dovetail, and you're off to a solid start.

6

Rope Care

In 1986, I stepped off a 500-foot-high tower in Arches National Monument, Utah. I thought I was clipped to the rappel rope, but I wasn't. I free-fell 160 feet before a spare 9-millimeter haul line clipped to my gear sling wadded itself into a knot and snagged in a fortuitous crack, like a cork in a bottle. The impact bent a carabiner and exploded the sheath off the rope. In some places, the core strands were nearly snapped in two. Obviously, that rope was ready for retirement. What about yours?

Climbing ropes demand attention. New ropes are especially fussy, prone to twisting and kinking. To remove kinks, uncoil the rope and pull its entire length through your hands several times. Letting the rope hang its full length down a wall will also remove twists. Repeat

An unpadded rope can become damaged and unsafe when sawed over a rough edge.

A padded rope.

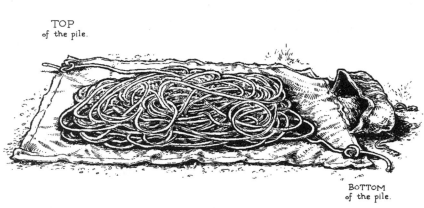

TOP
of the pile.

BOTTOM
of the pile.

Rope tarp.

as necessary, which will be often if you treat your rope to the Munter Hitch or Lap Coil.

Your rope will naturally soften as it breaks in, but you must be on guard, as many evils will conspire to destroy it. The common foils are sharp rock, dirt, ultraviolet (UV) light, and certain chemicals. Avoid sharp rock by picking a line that lets the rope track away from the hungry edges. When this isn't possible, use runners to draw the rope away from edges. Be especially careful when you are "fixing" a rope or rigging it for a top rope. Climbers have died because of the sawing action of a loaded rope. Pad, tape over, or hammer down any sharp or rough spots the rope might rub over. And remember, it doesn't take much to cut a loaded rope.

Dirt, besides griming up your hands and clothes, causes internal abrasion in your rope. Don't throw your rope on the ground, and don't step on it. Use a rope tarp to keep your rope as clean as possible. Many models of rope tarps are available; the best roll up, burrito-style, and have padded carrying straps. Rope bags are doubly good, as they not only keep the rope clean, but because you keep the rope flaked loose inside them, they also eliminate coiling, and thus kinking, the rope.

Most climbers needn't worry about the degrading effects of UV light, simply because their ropes are never in the sun long enough to hurt them. Still, you can't be too careful. Store your rope in the shade, and use any sun-bleached fixed rope with extreme caution.

The common chemicals that will destroy your rope are sulfuric (battery) acid, chlorine, and bleach. Since your rope is most likely to contact these chemicals when it is in storage or being transported, always pack your rope in a rope tarp or bag. Contrary to what you may think, oil does not damage a climbing rope, which is made of oil. Oil does, however, attract dirt.

Battery acid, as well as other chemicals, can damage a rope.

WASHING A ROPE

Even if you take all the precautions, your rope will eventually get filthy. When that happens, wash it, but do so carefully. The best way is to uncoil your rope, then weave it into an Electrician's Braid. The braid will keep the rope from tangling or getting damaged in the wash. Next, drop the rope in a washing machine. If you

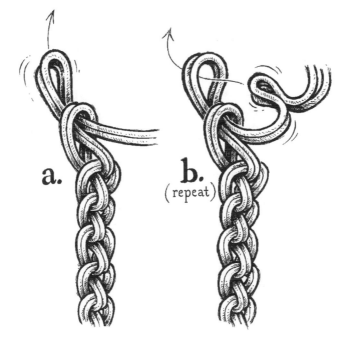

a.

b.
(repeat)

Electrician's Braid.

suspect that the previous load contained rope-eating bleach (always the case at a Laundromat), run the machine through a rinse cycle before washing the rope. Set the machine to delicate cycle and cold water (hot water will shrink the rope). Add a gentle soap, such as Ivory Snow. Do not use a detergent, which will strip the rope of its necessary oils (detergents always say "detergent" on the label). Let the rope run through a wash and rinse cycle. Then undo the braid and let the rope dry in a cool, shady place. Drying can take several days to a week, so plan ahead.

Those of you without access to a washing machine can simply pile the loose rope in a tub, add soap, and then get in and stomp the rope with your bare feet. Pretend you're crushing grapes for a hearty Bordeaux. Change the dirty water and repeat without soap until the water is clear and doesn't foam.

You may find that your aging rope is beginning to feel stiff and dry. That's because the factory treatment has worn or washed off. To restore that original supple feel, add fabric softener to the rinse when you wash your rope.

ROPE LIFE

The rope manufacturer Blue Water suggests retiring an unused climbing rope after five years. In practice, your rope, if you climb only on weekends, will likely need replacing every couple years. Active climbers may need a new rope every six months. Then again, a brand new rope may last only a day if it's been rent across a sharp edge.

How do you know when your rope is ready for the trash? The fact that you are thinking about it may be reason enough. A badly abraded sheath is another obvious clue. If the sheath is so worn that you can see the core, it's time for a new rope. Flat or mushy spots in your rope are other signs of fatal damage. Inconsistent rope diameter is another; if your rope has thick or thin places or feels lumpy, get a new one. Any chemical contact dooms a rope, as does a severe fall or melted spots, the consequence of reckless rappeling.

CUTTING ROPE, CORD, AND WEBBING

To cut a climbing rope, wrap the spot where you plan to cut with a band of masking or duct tape, then use a sharp knife (scissors saw and fray the rope) to cut through the tape and rope. The tape will prevent the rope from unraveling and make for a clean cut. Seal the rope end with a lighter. Heat the end until it's gummy, and form it into a nice,

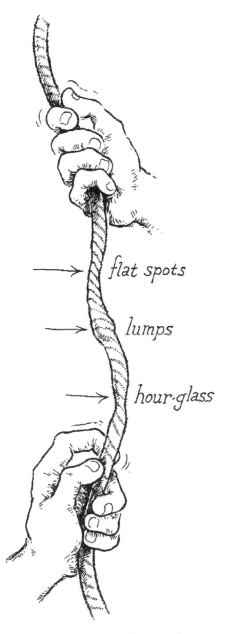

flat spots

lumps

hour-glass

Signs of a worn or damaged rope.

sealed casing. Rough and high spots will crack and fray; take care to do a clean job. Cut webbing and cord the same way, but you can do without the tape and use sharp scissors in place of the knife.

When a knife or scissors aren't at hand, such as on a climb, you can cut rope, cord, or webbing by bashing it apart with a sharp rock, hammering it over an edge, or chopping it in two with a knifeblade piton. Pulling the rope, sling, or cord tight makes the cutting go faster (a bad thought when you are rappeling or jumaring). Crude, but effective.

THROWING A ROPE

I'm including a bit on throwing a rope down a cliff because I've watched too many climbers make a mess of it and spend pointless effort—sometimes risky effort—straightening things out. No doubt many overnight epics owe themselves to the bungled rope throw.

The first thing to get straight is that you should never pitch off the rope without first checking that the end is tied to the anchors. Sounds basic, but you'd be surprised at how many climbers assume their partners have secured the ends, when they haven't. Make it a point to always check this yourself, even if your partner says he has done so.

After ensuring that the rope is anchored, stack the rope loose on the ground, with the anchor portion on the bottom and the end on top. Never throw off the entire rope. Instead, throw the rope down in sections, starting with the tail. A bulky Stopper Knot tied in the end will help the rope fall straight. When you have two ropes, toss them down one at a time, again making sure they are tied together and run through the anchor.

The above technique will work in most situations, unless there is high wind. Then, a thrown rope will likely blow around—sometimes straight up—and snag behind a flake. Avoid this distressing scenario by loosely tucking the rope, ends first, in a pack. Have the first person down wear the pack, leaving it open so that the rope can unwind a bit at a time. Once the first person is down, he should retain the rope ends and hold the rope steady for the second person.

7

On Cord

We don't think much about cord, yet use it almost as often as the rope, and like the rope, we depend on it absolutely.

Cord is the small stuff we thread through nuts and use to fashion Prusiks and occasionally runners. Useful diameters are 3 to 9 millimeters. Cord, also called perlon, is made the same as kernmantle lead rope, and in the case of the 8- to 9-millimeter diameters, it is lead rope wound onto spools. Three- to 5-millimeter cord makes good shoelaces and keeper cords for nut tools, hammers, drills, and so on. Five- to 7-millimeter cord is ideal Prusik material, but certain 5.5- and 7-millimeter are designed just for slinging nuts and are braided from special high-strength and hard-to-cut Spectra or Kevlar yarns. Given a choice between the two, get Spectra. Kevlar, while bulletproof, weakens with repeated flexing, much like clothes hanger wire. Spectra holds up better. Do not use Spectra or Kevlar for Prusiks—it is too stiff to grip the rope. Some big-wall climbers use 7-millimeter cord for haul lines. It's lightweight but painful to grip and gives a fast and hot rappel, should the need arise.

Do much trad, ice, or wall climbing, and you will thank the *cordalette* every time you rig a belay. The cordalette is a loop made from 20 feet of 7-millimeter cord tied with a Double Fisherman's. In use, you clip the cordalette through each point of protection, gather together a loop from each point, and tie these together with a Figure Eight on a Bight. Clip into the Figure Eight with two carabiners, gates reversed and opposed, or locking.

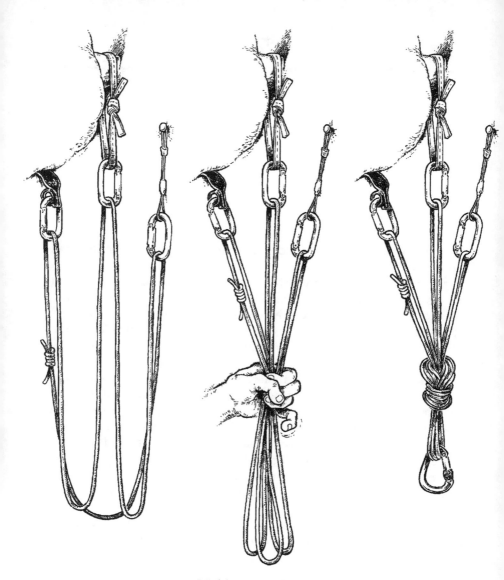

Making a cordalette.

The beauty of the cordalette lies in its ability to self-equalize the anchor. Strung properly, each anchor bears an equal load, and should one anchor fail, the others will be spared a shock load. Besides being near foolproof, lightweight, compact, and practical, the cordalette spares the full end of the lead rope for leading. You can construct an adequate cordalette from either regular 7-millimeter cord or the better, stronger, and tougher 7-millimeter Spectra.

Both Spectra and Kevlar require feats of strength and patience to cut. Wire nippers are the most effective; scissors and knives do as much fraying as cutting. Once you sever the cord, you must seal the ends. To do this, pull the sheath back ¾ inch or so, and trim the core a fraction shorter than the sheath. Pull the sheath over the shortened core, and use a lighter to melt the end into a blunt cap. Use the same method to cut regular nylon cord, although here a knife or sharp scissors will work fine.

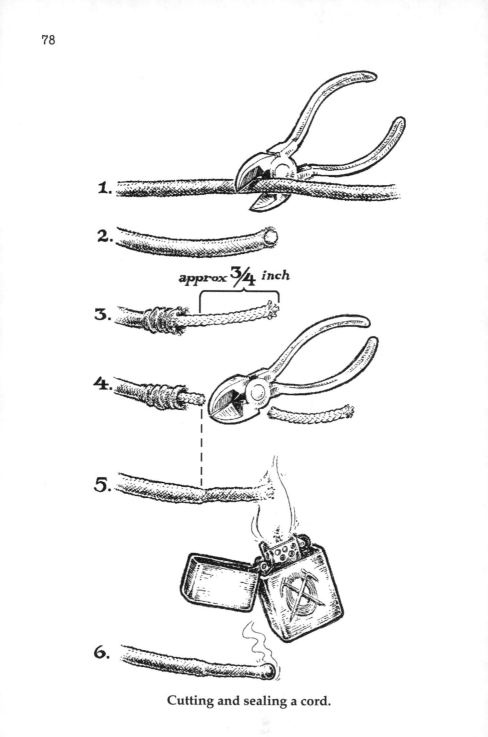

approx **3/4** inch

Cutting and sealing a cord.

8

On Webbing

Webbing is the central character in the rope-to-protection chain. It forms the quickdraws we clip to bolts, the runners we clip to cams and nuts, and we thread it through fixed anchors to rig rappels. Our harnesses are made of it. So are aiders, daisy chains, and tie-offs. We even use it to sling water bottles.

If there are dozens of ways to use webbing, there are also dozens of types of webbing. The two you should concern yourself with are flat and tubular. Flat webbing is just as it sounds, flat and one-dimensional. Seat belts are a good example of flat webbing. So are certain nylon belts. The disadvantages of flat webbing are that it cuts and abrades more easily and is about half as strong as tubular. Its advantages are that it is lighter in weight and less bulky than tubular. For those reasons, flat webbing makes the best aiders and sewn goods, such as harnesses and quickdraws. For regular knotted products, such as runners, however, tubular webbing is superior.

Tubular webbing is woven round, like Chinese handcuffs or tube socks. Its multi-

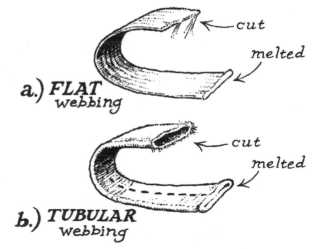

Cross sections of flat and tubular webbing.

sided design makes it very strong and durable for its width. For that reason, it is always the webbing of choice. You must be careful, though, when selecting tubular webbing, as there is good stuff and bad.

The best tubular webbing is woven into a continuous loop, similar to the sheath on a climbing rope. Avoid the type that is woven flat, then folded into a tube and stitched down the edge. Snag or cut the edge seam, and the tube falls apart. Surplus stores still carry spools of this seamed webbing, but it is getting more difficult to find in climbing shops. Just as well.

Common tubular webbing widths are ½-inch, ⁹⁄₁₆-inch, 1-inch, and 2-inch. Flat webbing is typically 1-inch and 2-inch.

TIE-OFFS
Half-inch tube is the weakest, but it's the most supple and cinches down the best, making it the top material for tying off pitons. Make your tie-offs from 2 feet of webbing, and tie the ends with a water knot. Seal the cut ends with a lighter to prevent them from unraveling.

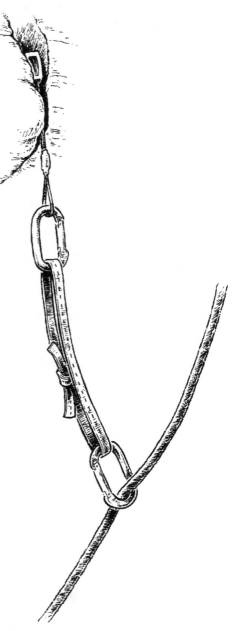

Clipping a runner to the protection and the rope can decrease the chances of dislodging the placement.

Half-inch tie-offs are delicate and prone to cutting. You may get only one use per tie-off, especially if you put the tie-off on a piton and then drive the pin in a corner. Even in top shape, a ½-inch tie-off breaks at just over 1,000 pounds. When they are nicked, they can break at half that weight. Use them carefully, and inspect them often. Retire frayed tie-offs. I put two and sometimes three tie-offs on critical pieces. On a big aid climb like El Capitan in Yosemite, you'll use fifty to a hundred or more tie-offs. Free climbers will seldom if ever need even one.

RUNNERS

Runners are the open loops used for a myriad of chores. Wear one bandolier-style over your shoulder, and it becomes a functional, albeit painful, gear sling. Clip a runner to your protection and then the rope, and the flop and tension of the rope are less likely to dislodge the placement. Girth Hitch a runner to your harness, and you can clip yourself to belay or rappel anchors. Twist a runner into a figure eight, and it becomes a pair of emergency leg loops or a daisy chain. The uses are endless.

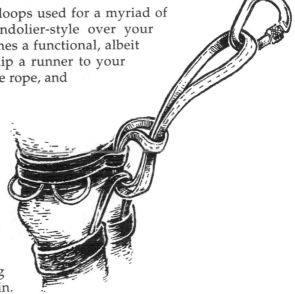

Runner girth hitched to a harness.

Common runners are the single and double. *Single runners* are tied in loops from 6 to 7 feet of ⁹⁄₁₆-inch tubular webbing. You can tie runners from 1-inch tubular webbing, but the wider webbing is bulkier and more difficult to work with. Use the Ring Bend to tie your runners. Tie each loop, then hook it to a stout tree limb, clip a stirrup or aider to the loop, and bounce your body weight on it to draw the knot up tight. A wet knot gives the tightest set. As a final precaution, you can tape the tails to the loop. Stitching also works but is difficult to undo when you find yourself in a tight spot and in need of a single length of webbing. Inspect your Ring Bends before each use, and retie if they have gone soft or the tails have shortened.

Runner used as an emergency pair of leg loops.

You can use buy sewn runners, which are slightly stronger and sleeker than knotted ones, but you can't untie and thread them through fixed anchors, tunnels in the rock, or around trees. Whichever sort you prefer, wear them on your shoulder, cartridge-belt-style.

The number of single runners you'll need depends on the sort of climbing you're going to do. Sport climbers will need only two for anchoring at belay, lower, or rappel stations, whereas big-wall climbers can need twenty. As runners are inexpensive and lightweight, it's better to carry too many than too few.

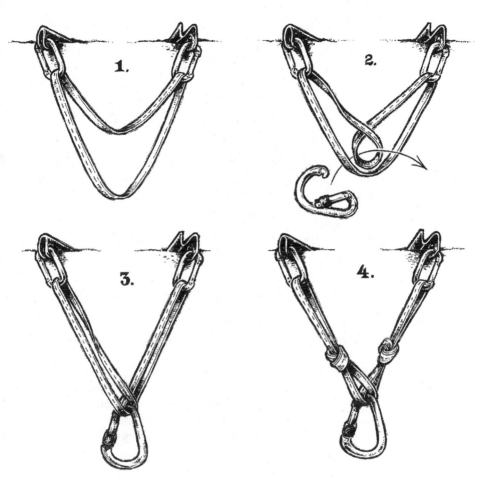

A double runner used to equalize two anchors. Note that you must secure each side of the sling with an Overhand on a Bight (step 4) in order to prevent a shock load should one of the anchors fail.

Double runners are twice (or three times) as long as single runners and are used mostly to string together belay, rappel, and top-rope stations. A couple of these are usually adequate for any situation. If you use your long runners primarily for top-roping, make them from 1-inch tubular webbing, which cuts less readily than the thinner stuff.

Quickdraw.

QUICKDRAWS

Quickdraws are short, 4- to 6-inch straps of webbing used to clip bolts, or nuts or cams when the line is straight and rope drag won't be a problem. You can tie quickdraws from a couple feet of %₆-inch tubular webbing, but since quickdraws are too short to thread through anything anyway, the less bulky sewn versions are superior. Sewn quickdraws are usually made from flat webbing and have a rubber band or gasket to trap the bottom carabiner. Most sport climbers own about two dozen quickdraws.

DAISY CHAINS

Wall climbers will often find that they need to fix themselves to an anchor, usually to hang from it, but need to do so without tying up the rope. The daisy chain is built for just such a need. This 3- to 6-foot length of %₆-inch webbing has pockets every 2 inches for its entire length. Girth Hitch the daisy chain through the leg loops and belt of your harness, and you have a row of convenient attachment points. Since you usually anchor to two pieces of protection, permanently fix two daisy chains to your harness.

To make a daisy chain, purchase 20 feet of %₆-inch tubular webbing. Tie the ends together with a Ring Bend. Leave the tails long and tape them so they never work free. Next, grab both sides of the loop, and tie a series of Overhands every 2 inches. Make one side of each forming pocket slightly longer than the other so you clip into the thing when the daisy chain is pulled taut.

AIDERS

Aiders, or webbing ladders, are another indispensable item for the aid climber. These you can buy sewn, usually from 1-inch flat webbing, or you can tie your own from the same stock. Thinner webbing is lighter and less bulky, and although it's ideal for alpine and speed climbing, it wears too quickly to give good service to enthusiastic wall climbers. Aiders come in four- and five-step versions. I like the five-step and carry four for all but the easiest climbing. The best commercial aiders have "grab" loops at the clip-in pocket and reinforced steps that stay open when the aider is weighted. Clip two aiders to one carabiner, and you'll always have a step for each foot.

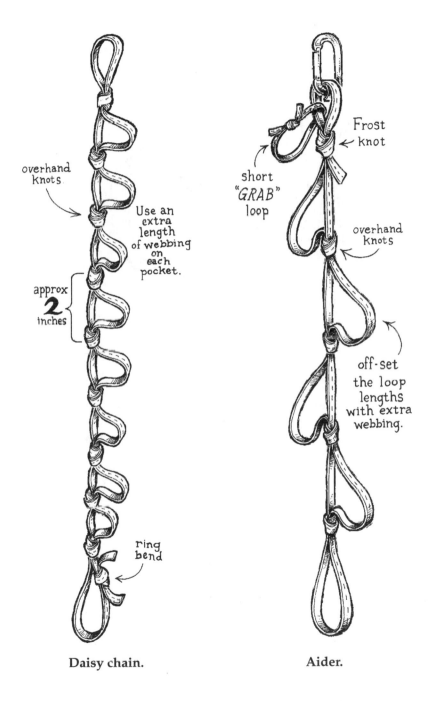

overhand
knots

Use an
extra
length
of webbing
on
each
pocket.

approx
2
inches

ring
bend

Frost
← knot

short
"GRAB"
loop

overhand
knots

off-set
the loop
lengths
with extra
webbing.

Daisy chain.

Aider.

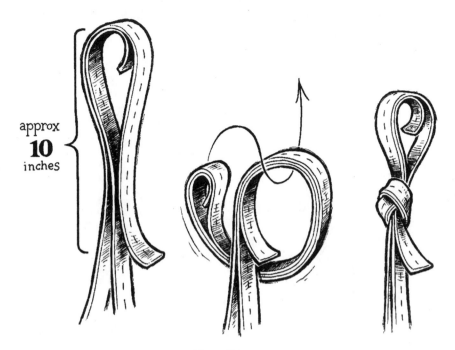

approx
10
inches

Frost Knot.

If you want to tie your own aiders, do so as follows for each aider:
1. Purchase 16 feet of 1-inch, flat webbing.
2. Tie the ends with a Frost Knot. Leave the tails long, and tape them down.
3. Use the Ring Bend to tie a short clip-in loop at the top of the aider.
4. Use the Overhand on a Bight to tie five large steps. Leave one side of each loop longer than the other so that the step hangs open when the aider is weighted.

GLOSSARY

belay: to secure a person or an object with rope.

belay plate or device: a slotted metal (usually aluminum) device that cinches onto the rope to provide friction for belaying, lowering, or rappeling.

bend: a knot that ties two rope, cord, or webbing ends together.

bight: the slack length of rope between its two ends.

carabiner: snap-links, typically of aluminum, although steel is common for use in high-wear situations, such as indoor gyms. Carabiners come in various shapes, the most common of which are the oval, D, modified D, and HMS (pearabiner). They may be nonlocking or locking.

CEN: a European testing organization; similar to the UIAA.

cinch: to pull a knot tight.

cord: slang for rope, but also used to describe perlon, or rope smaller than 9 millimeters in diameter.

cordage: all rope and cord, but originally applied only to twist-construction rope.

cordalette: a large loop of 7-millimeter cord used primarily to equalize belay anchors.

core: the center of a kernmantle rope. Also called the *kern.*

daisy chain: a loop of webbing with pockets tied or sewn throughout its length to provide numerous anchor points.

double rope: a rope designated by the UIAA or CEN as safe for lead climbing only when used in double strands. Both strands of a double rope need not be clipped to every protection point. Do not confuse double ropes with twin ropes.

dynamic rope: a rope designed to stretch. All climbing ropes are dynamic to absorb much of the impact generated in a fall.

fall factor: the number used to determine the severity of a fall, determined by dividing the distance of the fall by the amount of rope that catches that fall. The higher the number, the harder the fall. A 20-foot fall on 10 feet of rope has a fall factor of 2 (20 feet divided by 10 feet).

falls held: the number of UIAA or CEN test falls that a rope can sustain before breaking. Each UIAA test fall has a fall factor of 1.78.

finish: to pull a knot taut. Unfinished or loose knots are dangerous, as they can come untied and are weaker than finished knots.

flake or flake out: to loosely stack an uncoiled rope so it can pay out without snarling.

flat webbing: webbing that is manufactured flat, as opposed to tubular. Flat webbing is common in harnesses, but otherwise is seldom used for climbing.

hand: the "feel" of a rope—stiff or soft.

hawser: a large-diameter laid or twisted rope. Not applicable to climbing or rappeling.

hitch: a knot that secures a rope to an object, which can include another rope.

kern: see *core*.

kernmantle: a two-part rope construction having a braided or twisted core, the *kern,* and a braided sheath, the *mantle.* Climbing ropes are exclusively of kernmantle construction.

Kevlar: a high-strength fiber used in cord.

laid rope: rope with a twisted construction. Ropes of this sort are no longer used for climbing but are still popular with sport rappels. Typically, the core of a kernmantle rope has a laid construction.

mantle: a kernmantle rope's braided covering or sheath.

maximum impact force: the peak force generated in a fall. By UIAA standards, the maximum allowed is 2,640 pounds for single and twin ropes and 1,760 pounds for double ropes.

nip: the pressure, or binding, point in a knot that prevents it from slipping.

pay out: to feed or slack out rope.

perlon: nylon rope, but usually meant to describe kernmantle cord under 9 millimeters in diameter.

quickdraw: a short length of webbing (usually 6 inches or less) with a loop stitched or tied into each end.

rappel: to slide down a rope.

rope bag: a sack, usually nylon, used to store a rope. Most rope bags also have a built-in tarp that keeps the flaked rope out of the dirt.

runner: a loop of tied webbing, although you can use cord or rope, usually long enough to be worn over the shoulder bandolier-style.

set: to tighten a knot.

sheath: a kernmantle rope's braided covering. Also called the *mantle*.

single rope: a dynamic climbing rope designated by the UIAA or CEN as safe for single-strand lead use.

sling: any tied or sewn loop of webbing or cord.

Spectra: a high-strength fiber used in cord.

static elongation: the amount a rope will stretch under a 176 pound load. This specification is in reality of little useful purpose.

static rope: a rope with little or no stretch. Rope of this sort is commonly used for rappeling, spelunking, and "fixing" on big walls. Static rope should never be used for climbing, as it lacks the ability to absorb the impact force generated in a fall.

stopper knot: any bulky knot tied in the end of a rope. Usually used to prevent rappeling off the end of the rope.

supertape: a type of thick, tubular webbing, usually ⁹⁄₁₆ inch wide.

tie-offs: short loops of tied webbing (6 inches or less) used to hitch over pitons to reduce leverage.

tubular webbing: webbing that is woven with a circular, or tubular, construction. Since tubular webbing is double sided, it is generally stronger and more durable than flat webbing of equal width.

twin rope: a rope designated by the UIAA or CEN as safe for lead climbing only when it is used in double strands and both strands are clipped to every point of protection. Do not confuse twin ropes with double ropes. A single strand of double rope will withstand a fall; a single strand of twin rope will not.

UIAA: the Union Internationale des Association d'Alpinisme, an international body that sets guidelines for climbing equipment and testing.

waterproof or dry treatments: the coating given a rope to minimize water absorption. Some coatings are topical, or applied after manufacturing to the sheath only; superior treatments are applied during manufacture, so that each fiber is individually coated. Typically, such coatings make a rope softer and less prone to kinking than a nontreated rope. Coatings also make a rope slicker, improving durability.

whipping: to tape, melt, or otherwise seal the end of a rope to prevent fraying.

About the Author and Illustrator

Duane Raleigh has been climbing since 1973. He has climbed extensively throughout the United States, including several solo ascents of Yosemite's El Capitan. This is his fourth book on the sport, the others being *Rock, Tools and Technique; Ice, Tools and Technique;* and *Clip and Go.* He was the equipment editor for *Climbing* magazine from 1990 to 1996 and is currently the editor for the same publication. Duane lives in the Rocky Mountains near Marble, Colorado, with his wife, Lisa.

Mike Clelland has illustrated six climbing books, two camping books, and a "really cool" backcountry ski book. Mike never went to art school, studying *Mad Magazine* instead. He grew up in the very flat state of Michigan and spent the historic 1980s as a yuppie in New York City. Mike was introduced to climbing in the last stronghold of "traditional" technique, the Gunks. Finding it impossible to ignore an eco-groovy voice down deep in his soul, Mike moved to Wyoming and began working as an instructor for the National Outdoor Leadership School (NOLS) and doing an occasional cartoon for *Climbing* magazine. Mike is presently living in a shed in Idaho.